Let Sleeping Cats Lie

Pet Poems

Also available by Brian Bilston

50 Ways to Score a Goal and other football poems

Refugees

Let Sleeping Cats Lie

Pet Poems

Brian Bilston

MACMILLAN CHILDREN'S BOOKS

Published 2024 by Macmillan Children's Books
an imprint of Pan Macmillan
The Smithson, 6 Briset Street, London EC1M 5NR
EU representative: Macmillan Publishers Ireland Ltd, 1st Floor,
The Liffey Trust Centre, 117–126 Sheriff Street Upper
Dublin 1, D01 YC43
Associated companies throughout the world
www.panmacmillan.com

ISBN 978-1-0350-5055-0

1 3 5 7 9 8 6 4 2

A CIP catalogue record for this book is available from the British Library.

Printed and bound by CPI Group (UK) Ltd, Croydon CR0 4YY

In loving memory of Buttons.
Sleep well, our beautiful cat.

Contents

Pet Poem

Do you have a pet poem,
one which never leaves your side?
Words to whisper to yourself
or shout out loud with pride?

A poem that is yours alone
on which you can depend?
That's always there when you feel down,
a loyal and faithful friend?

A poem that's a part of you
to carry in your heart –
that's funny, sad, or makes you think,
that's inspirational or smart?

A poem is a precious pet;
there are lots of different kinds.
Treat it well and the love you give
gets repaid ten thousand times.

A Polite Request

Dad, I want a cat. I *really* want a cat.
Please can we get a cat?
All my friends have got a cat. All of them!
So can we get one, too? Can we? Can we? Can we?
Please, please, please!

Oh, I'd do anything for a cat, I really would.
Please, Dad. I will clean your car every day.
I will put my clothes in the laundry basket.
I will make you a cheese sandwich.
Please can we get a cat?

Dad, please, can we get a cat?
Just a small one. You'd barely notice it.
It would hardly take up any room –
they're only about the same size as a small dog
or a very large mouse. *Pleeeeeasse!*

Dad? I was learning today at school
about how pets can be brilliant for your mental health
and I suddenly thought: A CAT! THAT'S IT!
WHY DON'T WE GET A CAT?! The idea just came
to me like that! What do you think?

Dad, have you heard about the news?
There's a crimewave apparently. Sounds serious.
What if somebody was to break into our house?
We should get a guard cat. You know, who's scary,
but also really soft and cuddly and cute.

Cough, cough. Dad, I think this is it . . .
it's all over for me. *Cough, cough.*
Doctor says the only thing which can save me – *cough* –
is some kind of small domesticated mammal
with soft fur and retractable claws. *Cough.*

Dad, plllllllllllleeeeeeeeeeeeeeeeeeeeeeeeeeee-
eeeeeeeeeeeeeeeeeeeeeeeeeeeeeeeeeeeeee-
eeeeeeeeeeeeeeeeeeeeeeeeeeeeeeeeeeeeee-
eeeeeeeeeeeeeeeeeeeeeeeeeeeeeeeeeeeeee-
eeeeeeeeeeeeeeeeeeeeeeeeeeeeeeeeeeeeee-

eeeeeaaaassssssssssse! What's that?
You've *got* me a cat? Over there . . . in that basket?
Oh, would you look at her! She's adorable! I *love* her!
What? No, sorry, can't feed her or play with her
at the moment, I'm off to Lucy's house.

4

Wilf the Labracadabrador

Wilf the Labracadabrador
(who in dog years is seventy-six)

is a magician, a conjurer
and a hypnotist.

He saws teddies in half.
He pulls rabbits from hats.

He makes all his food vanish,
just like that.

Renowned for his showdogship
and smooth sleight of paw,

Wilf's about to em-bark
on a nationwide tour.

Last week, I showed him
how to juggle with sticks.

Whoever said you can't teach
an old dog new tricks?

Memories of a Goldfish

'Goldfish do have good memories, scientists find.'
BBC News

I guess by now you've heard the news –
how I wish it wasn't true!

It's no wonder I feel miserable,
you'd find it boring, too –

swim swim swimming all day long,
with nothing much to do.

If only I could just forget,
what excitement would ensue –

with each circuit of my bowl,
to find everything is new!

On '„„;;pppppp'[[[[[[[[[[;':
///////////////////////3,'

Upon returning to my desk,
having left it temporarily in search of biscuits,
I discovered my cat had written
another poem on my laptop.

It was called '„„;;pppp
 pp'[[[[[[[[[[;';///////////////////////3,'
and while it constituted one of her more difficult pieces,
it was also the kind of poem
which rewarded repeat reading.

I was struck by its experimental structure,
the absence of line breaks;
indeed, not one single space
between any of the poem's 10,000 or so characters.

One of the work's central motifs –
'jjjjjjjjjjjjjjjjjjjjjjjjjjjjjjjjjjjjjjjjjjjjkkkkkkkkkkkkkkkkkkkkkk' –
was, by turns, reassuring and unsettling,
while the symbolism of '##################'

hinted at our twenty-first-century preoccupation
   with social media.
And yes, there were perhaps a few elements
which did not work: twelve whole pages
containing just the number 7 seemed a little excessive,

while her introduction of the character T
was not altogether convincing. But who could not be
   moved
by that devastating final line, its message of hope
piercing our hearts like an arrow: 333333333333333,,,

Two's Company, Flea's a Crowd

we used to be happy,
my doggy & me,
until that fateful day
he befriended a flea

& now when I take my doggy to the park
he doesn't want to chase a stick
he tells me it's not his shtick
any more

it's such a bore, he says,
lying down in the grass with his new friend, Flea,
to discuss matters of mathematics
astrophysics & philosophy

& when I throw his ball for him to catch
he says, no thanks, I'm fine,
I'm playing 'I'll Scratch Your Back, You Scratch Mine'
with Flea, you see

& when I suggest we race to that tree,
he says, sorry, but I promised Flea
we'd do some jumping about for a bit,
he's very good at it, you know

& when I tell my doggy he's gonna get hurt,
that he's just being used,
Flea's a blood-sucking parasite,
my doggy says, Don't be daft! Flea's alright!

besides Flea's my mate, and what's a bite
or two between old pals?
none of us is perfect is his rationale,
least of all *you*, he says,

shocked, I say what do you mean?
& he says, well, just look at you,
you're having a pet
about your pet having a pet

you're practically green with envy,
worked yourself up into a frenzy,
when you need to be more friendly
then you'll see

so I gave it a go
I joined in their games & debates
& it wasn't long
before some of Flea's mates

started to hang out with me
until my fears all disappeared
& I was finally at ease
just me & my doggy (& two hundred fleas)

Pet Peeve

Keeping
a chameleon
for a pet

is something
that I now
regret.

At first,
as far as
I could tell,

he seemed
to blend in
very well,

but he's
changed a lot
in many ways

I've not
seen him now
for fourteen days.

Alarm Cat

Before going to bed,
I always remember to make sure
to set my alarm cat
for the following day.

Sure enough, every morning –
a few short hours before it's time to get up –
my alarm cat wakes me,
by sitting on my head.

Watering the Flowers

A short poem written by my dog

Roses are grey
Violets are grey
I cock my leg
And give them a spray

Ten Reasons Why It's Inadvisable to Keep a Blue Whale as a Pet

1. Blue whales are famously opinionated and argumentative. In fact, they're always spouting off about something or other.

2. It can be hard locating your breakfast cereal in the morning because the food cupboard is full of krill.

3. They take up all the sofa.

4. Their powerful flippers can be problematic when high-fiving, and may result in you being flung into a nearby wall.

5. Blue whales frequently snore in their sleep, which may upset your neighbours up to ten miles away.

6. They have shocking table manners, and will sit for long periods with their mouths wide open in the hope their food will just float in.

7. Blue whales are – by nature – solitary creatures and will often spend whole days in their bedrooms, listening to sad sea shanties and writing bad poetry.

8. Although blue whales have no teeth of their own, they will often leave the lid off the toothpaste because they 'feel like it'.

9. They can be hard to get into their carriers when it's time for the annual check-up at the vets.

10. While the song of the blue whale may be beautiful, they rarely put in the hours for violin practice and their ukulele playing is – quite frankly – awful.

Meanwhile . . .

I wish we could take them all home with us.
I hear that a lot. And I believe them, I really do.
But it's not practical, of course. I get that.
There'd be space issues, and the cost of keeping us all –
there must be twenty of us, at least – well,
it's never going to happen. And so they drive off,
back to their warm houses, their big gardens,
with the cutest, the youngest, the brightest of us,
secured in the middle seat between excited children.

Look at that old guy. Wonder how long he's been here?
I hear that a lot, too. I share their wonder these days.
But I like it here: people talk to me; I get fed;
fresh water every day; regular exercise. Before I came
    here . . .
well, let's just say that's not always been the case.
Here, though, they're kind to me. I'm learning how
    to love.
And, if I can learn enough, who knows, maybe one day
someone will peer through the mesh and say:
That one there, I've found him – I think he's the one.

17

Love Rat

He was a *rattus norvegcius domestica*
who went by the name of Stan
(although he would also answer to Colin)
and I was his biggest fan.

We were always in close proximity.
I was never more than six feet away from him
and he was never more
than six feet away from me.

He would sit on my shoulder on the bus,
without fanfare or fussiness,
while our fellow passengers screamed
instead of minding their own bussiness.

Rats get a bad rap. Not once did he
tell on me. He was never dishonest or dirty
and throughout the leaky ship of those teenage years,
he did not desert me

until one morning I went to wake him
to find myself predeceased.
I dug a grave in the garden. Made a sign.
RIP Stan (Colin). Rat in peace.

'Arry the 'Amster

Gotta problem you need sortin'?
Consignment of hay cubes you fancy exportin'?
Some seed 'n' nut mix you could do with extortin'?
Exercise wheel you wanna see brought in?
In a bit of a jam, sir? In need of a scamster?
You need . . . 'Arry the 'Amster

Ever wanna break out of yer cage?
Or need help with a Rat War you wanna wage?
Fancy getting your paws on a sweet bit of sage?
Well, 'ere's the geezer you should engage,
He's a dancer, he's a chancer
He's called . . . 'Arry the 'Amster

'Arry's got his paws in a lot of pies
He's the small mammalian master of deceit 'n' disguise
But should you ever meet 'im, one thing I'd advise:
Don't ever look 'im in his little beady eyes
Cos I tell you, he don't give a damn, sir
Not 'im . . . not 'Arry the 'Amster

Don't be fooled by his cute little squeak
His soft furry coat or his dwarfish physique
I'm tellin' you that little guy is a freak
Keeps a Kalashnikov inside his left cheek
Cos he's a villain, a gangster
A Jean-Claude Van Dammester
Whatever's yer question, this guy's the answer
Yeah, that's right
I'm talkin' 'bout 'Arry the 'Amster

On the Fly

Some kids have loads of pets
Some have none at all
As for me, the only one I've ever had
Is a fly on the wall

You might have heard about him from that documentary
There were three episodes in all
looking at his life before he ended up on the wall

The first showed him losing his temper with a doorknob
It caused quite a scandal
That one was called 'Fly off the Handle'

The next one found him messing around in the bathroom
Critics thought it was a bit of disappointment
It was called 'Fly in the Ointment'

The final episode, he was in my underwear drawer
Doing a silly dance
That one was called . . . yes, sorry, you guessed it . . .
'Fly by the Seat of my Pants'

The News Where I Am
(A Love Poem to My Dog)

Today, I called my teacher Mum.
Forgot my lunch. Messed up my sums.
Spent all playtime on my own
    but
        you'll be there when I get home.

Played rounders and I dropped a catch.
Found 'KICK ME' pinned onto my back.
My favourite book is out on loan.
    Who cares?
        You'll be there when I get home.

School play today, a chance to shine.
Tripped up on stage then fluffed my line.
I grazed my knee. I lost my phone.
    Like, whatever.
        You'll be there when I get home.

A pigeon pooped on my right shoe.
Think I'm coming down with flu.
It's been the most perfect day that I've known!
    Because
        – did I mention this? –
            you'll be there when I get home.

Meander

s
s
s
s
o then,
me and her,
her and me, we're
as happy as can be
I think my little
heart would
break, if
not for my
shiny-scaly
snake and
although
she might
give mum
the shivers
I love to
watch her
while she
slithers
around
in her
vivarium.
I tell you,
she's not
so scary,
mum!
x

Four-Legged Friend

Oh, my faithful four-legged friend,
you're the one on whom I depend.
You're somehow always there for me
at breakfast, dinner, lunch or tea.
Sturdy, loyal, strong and stable,
much beloved – my kitchen table.*

*Although walks in the park with you
are, frankly, no walk in the park.
They are, in fact, complete disasters –
how I wish that you had castors.

Do the Cat

A new dance craze is sweeping the nation
Everybody get down to the big sensation ...

Do the cat!
Yeah, do the cat!
Give your limbs a stretch & jump up on a lap
Close those eyes real tight & have a little nap
Do the cat!
Yeah, do the cat!

Is your day full of troubles? Do you need to de-stress?
Come on, then, do the cat – and grab a big snoozefest ...

Do the cat!
Yeah, do the cat!
Cancel all your plans & give those chores a skip
Curl up in a ball & get yourself some kip
Do the cat!
Yeah, do the cat!

It really doesn't matter if you're young or old
You know what to do, don't wait to be told

Do the cat!
Yeah, do the cat!
Curl up in a ball or collapse in a heap
Throw your cares aside & have a little sleep
Do the cat!
Yeah, do the cat!

Are you ready?
What!
I said, are you ready?
Say what!
I said, are you ready?
What's that!
Are you ready?
Let's do the cat! Oooooooohhhhhhhhhh . . .
Zzzzzzzzzzzzzzzzzzzzzzzzzzzzzzzzzzzzzzzzzzzzzzzzzz
zzzzzzzzzzzzzzzzzzzzzzzzzzzzzzzzzzzzzzzzzzzzzzzzzzz
zzzzzzzzzzzzzzzzzzzzzzzzzzzzzzzzzzzzzzzzzzzzzzzzzzz
zzzzzzzzzzzzzzzzzzzzzzzzzzzzzzzzzzzzzzzzzzzzzzzzzzz

You're doing the cat!
Yeah, that's the cat!
You're gettin' in the groove & you're doin' all the moves
You know what to do – now have a little snooze
Do the cat!
Yeah, do the cat!

Don't give me no rat
Don't give me no bat
Cos the cat is where it's at
Do the cat!
Do the cat!
Do the cat!
Do the ...
zzzzzzzzzzzzzzzzzzzzzzzzzzzzzzzzzzzzzzzzzzzzzzzzzzzz
zzzzzzzzzzzzzzzzzzzzzzzzzzzzzzzzzzzzzzzzzzzzzzzzzzzz
zzzzzzzzzzzzzzzzzzzzzzzzzzzzzzzzzzzzzzzzzzzzzzzzzzzz
zzzzzzzzzzzzzzzzzzzzzzzzzzzzzzzzzzzzzzzzzzzzzzzzzzzz

A Leisurely Walk

Reverend Ambrose McLeish,
devout man of the cloth,
prayed for a pet
and was delivered a sloth,

with whom he set out
for a walk round the block.
They departed the vicarage
at about two o'clock,

one fine afternoon
in the middle of May –
it's now late July
a   n   d
t   h   e   y   '   v   e
j   u   s   t
g   o   t
h   a   l   f   w   a   y   .

Meditations of Colin the Lugubrious Goldfish

I

I would rather be a big fish in a little pond
than a little pond in a big fish.

II

When you say, 'Give a man a fish and you feed him
    for a day;
teach a man to fish and you feed him for a lifetime,'
I say, 'Why are you encouraging this man to eat so
    many fish?
Some of them might be my friends.'

III

Ask yourself not how large is the tank
but how pretty is the ornamental treasure chest.

IV

Tomorrow is another day
although, chances are, it will be a lot like this one.

V

It is never too late to start over again,
except perhaps for Frank,
who has been floating at the top of the tank
for about half an hour now.

VI

Believe in yourself and you can do anything,
unless you're a goldfish,
in which case professional golfer may be beyond you.

VII

What goes around, comes around.
Oh look, there's that sunken pirate ship feature again.

VIII

It's not the taking part,
it's the swimming that counts.

IX

People need pets like a fish needs a bicycle,
and I *really* need a bicycle.

X

We are all in the fish tank,
but some of us are looking at the starfish.

Passwords

To make his passwords
harder to guess,
Graham would name them
after his pets –

his cats, Password1
and Password2,
and QWERTY123,
his cockapoo.

This budgerigar is not for budging

you'll never budge
my budgerigar
because his swing is the thing
he likes most by far

tempt him with crisps or fine caviar
offer him cake and a big fat cigar
you'll still never budge
my budgerigar

cos my little feathery geezer
is a dedicated, staunch trapezer,
more implacable than Julius Caesar –
weeny, beady, beaky,

a chappy who is cheeky,
a chatty, chirpy, chippy winger,
a charismatic bar-room singer,
a self-confessed steadfast swinger

who's not for budging
so do not judge him,
or attempt to nudge him,
or mildly begrudge him

just leave him be
and let him swing
watch him loop the loop
and hear him sing

oh, and while you're at it,
grab your guitar
and join in with the avian world's
most amazing star . . .

my loveable,
unbudgeable
budgerigar!

his name is Colin, by the way

What's in a Name?

The name had found her before we did.
She was called Buttons,
the man at the animal centre told us,
when we met her for the first time.
You can change it if you like, he said.

But we didn't. Buttons it would be,
we agreed, when we went back to get her:
she'd be used to it, we told ourselves;
she had enough to contend with already;
besides, she *looked* like a Buttons.

But, over the years, her name *did* change.
Buttsy, she'd be most often; also Buttles,
Buttsy Burger, Buttsy Malone. After gifting us
a live mouse, *Butthead!* we'd scream,
or sometimes just you silly cat.

Those occasions we'd transport her
on a cushion from one sofa to the other –
a journey for which she'd reserve her most regal
and imperious manner – it was only fitting
that she be The Empress of Buttonia.

But that last time, when we went to the vets
to collect her, to bring her back home again,
not this time in a strong and sturdy cat carrier
but in a small, heart-shaped silver urn,
she was Buttons once more, our Buttons.

Double L-pings

My Uncle Llewellyn
from south-west of Llanelli,
lliked all kinds of creatures,
but llamas especially.

He had llots and llots
on whom he'd llavish his time,
for they were lloyal and llarge-hearted;
Llewellyn thought them subllime.

How he lloved their llong necks,
their llaidback disposition,
with their lluxurious wool coats,
and their llanguid expressions.

A shame Uncle Llewellyn
was not llanguid as well –
I told him he llooked llike a llama,
he said go straight two l.

The Day My Dog Spontaneously Combusted

there he was,
chasing sticks,
doing tricks
and all that stuff

next minute, woof

Penguin Awareness

I've been aware of penguins since I was three:
I think one may have moved in with me.

The signs are everywhere.
The smell of saltwater in the air.
There are moulted feathers on my chair
Yesterday I found a fish upon the stair.
But when I turn around there's no one there,
for he moves in the shadows, like Tony Soprano;
I am forever stepping in guano.

I don't know why he's come to live with me.
There are better places for him to be.
But when I've gone to bed, I can hear the tread
of his soft heels across the kitchen floor,
and the opening of the freezer door.

And I picture him there,
his head resting on a frozen shelf,
dreaming sadly of somewhere else,
thinking about the hand that life has dealt him,
and I wonder if his heart is melting.

Let Sleeping Cats Lie

Please don't think me lazy,
I'm not trying to slack –
it's just that I'm stuck, you see,
under this cat.

I know there are jobs to do –
rooms to tidy, plates to stack –
only I'm a bit stuck, you see,
under this cat.

Yes, it is quite absurd
but she can't be disturbed
she'll get mildly perturbed,
and we can't have that –
so I guess I'd better stay
under this cat.

I would do my homework,
it's not application I lack –
problem is I'm stuck, you see,
under this cat.

I feel quite hungry now,
could you get me a snack?
The thing is I'm stuck, you see,
under this cat.

Yes, it is quite absurd
but she might get de-purred;
she really shouldn't be stirred
from her habitat –
so I guess I'd better stay
under this cat.

[Time passes ... minutes ... hours ... days ...
weeks ... months ... years ...
the cat yawns, stretches, jumps down,
wanders out into the garden]

That's twelve years of my life
I'll never get back
and all from being stuck
under that cat.

On the Chin

my dear long-eared pal,
shy & crepuscular,

you're fast & furrious,
athletic & muscular

a mighty muncher of hay,
a spin-wheel exponent,

a cage-climbing, run-jumping
fun-loving rodent

could I ever doubt you
by the merest scintilla?

not by the hairs
on my chinny chinchilla

Pet Phrases

My pet phrases get all mixed up
Don't believe me? Here's the proof –
This poem's a right cat's breakfast
I'm a dog on a cold tin roof

I may have been working like a cat
To try and put things right
But the dog has got my tongue
And it's not a pretty sight

My language has gone to the cats
I feel so stupid – silly me!
The cause of this hangcat expression –
I'm a complete dogastrophe

I set dogs among the pigeons
It's a cat eat cat world, I say
Curiosity, I claim, has killed the dog
And every cat must have its day

What on earth's a copy dog?
Hot diggety cat, it's such a drag
No wonder I'm in the cathouse
I let the dog out of its bag

Enough of such shaggy cat stories
It's driving me bananas
Oh I wish I could be more like you –
Because you're the dog's pyjamas

Weighty Matters

An auntie of mine,
(who shall remain anonymous)
was given a baby
hippopotamus.

When he was little,
she'd carry him everywhere –
to the shops, the playground,
the old village square,

and with each passing day,
he'd get a bit heavier,
while Auntie's arms grew achier,
her legs unsteadier,

and yet still she'd carry him
all over the town –
until that terrible day
she had him put down.

Ruminations of a Dog upon his Morning Walk

Of course, one does it for *their* benefit, not for one's own. Believe you me, I'd far rather be at home right now, reading an improving work of non-fiction or making progresswith today's crossword but the exercise is good for themand quite frankly they don't get enough of it, glued as they areto their phones and laptops all day. And one recalls the teachings of the noble ancient philosopher Dogrates who postulated that in order to exercise the mind, one must first exercise the body, and so this walk is not without its own usefulness to a canine of discernment . . . oh excuse me, I need to sniff this lamp post for a little while . . .

sniff, sniff, sniff, sniff, sniff, ooh yeah, mmm, sniff, sniff, sniff, sniff, sniff . . .

Sorry, where was I? Ah yes, this perambulation and the benefits therein. Of course, one has to *pretend* one likes it and make a big fuss whenever the word 'walkies' is mentioned, jump up and down, spin round a bit, get the old tail wagging like an out-of-control windscreen wiper. They seem to expect it, I don't know why. And, quite frankly, if it wasn't for that ridiculous pantomime, I doubt they would ever bother to leave the house at all. It's a wonder they don't . . . sorry, hang on, another lamp post . . .

sniff, sniff, sniff, sniff, sniff, ooh yeah, baby! mmm, sniff, sniff, sniff, sniff, sniff . . .

But I'm not complaining. Like I say, it's good for me, too. The fresh air allows me to clear my head, think straight, consider the complexities of existence. Spend some time figuring out why we're here, what life is all about. It must also be said that some of my best ideas have come when I'm out on a walk: the Ultimate Bonzo Bone Detector©, for instance. That's something you'll be hearing a lot more about in the next year or two. It's going to revolutionize the way in which . . . just one moment, dog's bottom . . .

sniff, sniff, snuffle, snuffle, sniff, ooh yeah, mmm, sniff, sniff, snuffle, snuffle, sniff . . .

Anyway, like I say, these walks do help to get one's grey cells working, which is not always easy when you're stuck at home. Which reminds me, I really must bark at them about repurposing the shed into a 'Creative Hub'. I'm thinking beanbags, snuffle mats, treat balls etc. It will benefit us all and – who knows? – may even bring us closer as a family. Oh look, we're back! I suppose I should make myself look adorable so they stroke me for a while. It helps to reduce their stress and anxiety, don't you know. After that, it's crossword time – or maybe I'll just sit and chew my squeaky elephant for a bit.

Guppy Love

when Gussie –
Gill's beloved guppy – fell ill
(he was looking rather green around the gills),
she took him to a vet
specializing in tropical fish

who, in turn, passed Gussie over
to a young student –
an action Gill thought imprudent
and made her fret

because he was not a fully qualified
wet pet vet yet

Cat Trouble

My cat is turning to ever more
elaborate methods of catching that mouse.

It used to be that she'd lie silently
on the floor, stretched out like a rug,
her mouth a painted tunnel entrance,
in the hope the mouse might stroll
inadvertently inside

but these days, it's frying pans
and fishing rods, cymbals, sticks of dynamite.
She sets traps of cheese and hides
behind the sofa, raising up her mallet.
Nothing seems to work.

It's all these cartoons she watches.
When she's not busy listening to walls
with her stethoscope,
or online shopping for mechanical mice,
she sits there, in front of the TV,

replaying each scene, thinking
and plotting, sketching contraptions,
one paw reaching distractedly
for the large tub of popcorn
the mouse holds out beside her.

Rough! Rough!

she bought
a posh set of pencils

and after a quick bowl
of noodles,

sketched some pictures
of her dog

nothing much,
just a few labradoodles

Fluffy

I call him Fluffy
because he's got very fluffy ears
on his very fluffy head
& very fluffy toes
& some very fluffy legs

he's got a very fluffy tail
& a very fluffy brain
sometimes he gets even fluffier
when I dry him from the rain

& if all the above
wasn't good cause enough,
the other reason he's called Fluffy

is
that he's just
a piece
of fluff

(that I keep in my belly button)

Whenever the Doorbell Rings

whenever the doorbell rings
my dog stops his napping

springs out of his basket
& starts up his yapping

YAP! YAP! YAP! YAP! YAP!
YAP! YAP! YAP! YAP! YAP!

then he YAP! YAP! races
to the YAP! YAP! door

I don't YAP! YAP! know
what on earth YAP! YAP! for

I mean,
it's hardly ever for him

Requiem for a Vanished Rabbit

The morning I went into the garden
to find you not there, the wire mesh
of your hutch twisted and broken
by an uninvited visitor in the night-time,
a fox or badger, most likely,

I thought of all those mornings past
when you *were* there, dashing in
and out of your house in jubilation
at the sight of me or the prospect
of a new day and whatever it held,

while I, bleary-eyed and inconvenienced,
changed your water, laid fresh hay
for your bed, did not think for one moment
that I would ever miss all this, these
troublesome chores of duty and love.

Strange Creature

My cousin Pat
has an octopussy cat.

He has three hearts
and nine lives,
which is an average
of one heart
every three lives.

He has eight furry tentacles, too,
and has been known
to light up
whenever a dog comes near him.

But enough about my cousin Pat.
As for what the octopussy cat is like, I have no idea –
I've never met him.

Heavy Weather

yesterday,
it rained cats and dogs,

the whole kit
and caboodle,

spent the hours
pussyfooting around,

then stepped
in a poodle.

Pet Snail Hits the Trail

didn't take me long to pack / got my house upon my back / the less cargo the better, you see / for escargots, the likes of me / & now I'm off, I've had enough / I'd love to stay but, hey ho ... TOUGH! / gotta hit the trail & make some slime / I've done my time / get yourself another pet / I'm oozing off into the sunset / well, I would if it didn't take an age / two hours now & I've not left this page oh now, I have! / but I feel homesick /gonna head back home / double quick

A Short Introduction to the Doggish Language

Most languages, I'm a total fool
I'm bottom of my class at school
I ain't no good with grammar rules
But I tell you I'm bi-ling-u-al
                    Because I know Doggish

'Woof, woof, woof' is what you say
Ruff translation: 'Can we play?'
I get your ball – I've made your day
Who needs textbooks anyway?

French, I find très difficile
German, I just don't get that spiel
Spanish, I always make a meal (and I don't mean paella)
But, I'm telling you, it's no big deal
                    Because I speak Doggish

Your big eyes staring into at mine
That's an easy one to define
We Doggish speakers know these signs
I get your food – it's dinner time

Don't know where I got this knowledge
I've never been to canine college
Search me! I know not a sausage
About how it was I learned Doggage
                    Sorry, Doggish. I mean, Doggish

From the hall, you fetch your lead
You wag your tail and start to plead
Don't worry, now, I won't misread
My Doggish skills are up to speed

And we share another language, you and me:
it begins with 'l', then there's an 'o', 'v' and 'e'

Haiku Composed by My Dog while Looking Out of the Window at a Passing Cat

Woof woof woof woof woof
Woof woof woof woof woof woof woof
Woof woof woof woof woof

International Cats

International cats
assert their right to relax
in international laps
at any time of day or night.
If denied, they will cite
the Universal Declaration of Feline Rights.

International cats
sit on international mats
that proclaim WELCOME
in each of the world's languages.
International cats can sleep
in up to seven different languishes.

International cats,
proud flouters of human orders,
support cat comrades across borders.
They extend the paw of friendship
to cats who flee catastrophe,
terror and adversity.

LIBERTY, EQUALITY, CATERNITY!

See You Later

Auntie Val,
an art curator,

got herself
an alligator,

in the hope he'd become
her pal. He ate her.

Hay Dude

Hay Dude, I hope you're glad
No more bad pongs, your cage is cleaner
Remember the pepper stored in your cheeks
Before you then seek tonight's dinner

And any time you like to play, Hay Dude, just say,
I'll make you a ball out of these old socks
For you must know that you're the one who makes
    life fun
Don't hide away inside your shoebox

Hay Dude, I love your purr
And your soft fur when I get to hold you
Surrender your little guinea pig charms
And let these arms reach out, enfold you

Watch you go out and you come in, Hay Dude, you
    spin,
You race through the tunnels like a mad thing
And don't you know that I love you, Hay Dude, it's
    true,
So come here and sit upon my shoulder

Hay Dude, don't be so glum
Here's a chum, too – see how I pet her
The minute I let her into your pen
Then your new friend will make things better

Better better better better better better, oh!
Na na na nananana, nananana, Hay Dude (repeat x
    100) . . .

Higher Things

My cat don't care too much for politics
She don't think about no war
She rarely watches television
And thinks football is a bore
She got her mind on higher things

My cat don't use her mobile phone
She ducks out of DIY
She got no time for magazines
She never wants to play 'I spy'
She got her mind on higher things

My cat ain't into modern art
Or the great affairs of state
She don't care about stocks and shares
Or the change in interest rates
The only thing she's interested in is higher things

My cat's given up the saxophone
She's knocked croquet on the head
She's had it with her ballet class
All her comics lie unread
Cos she's got her mind on higher things

And when I say higher things,
I mean higher things
Like the thing
With the wings
Perching high up in that tree

Beneath which my cat
Has been sat
Since last Tuesday,
Half past three.

Dog, Ticked Off

Aarrgh! Help!
Can someone please
Remove this
Objectionable tick
Stuck under my fur – he's
Slowly sucking all
The life out of me,
Ill-tempered little mite. You got him?
Cheers! That's so very
Kind of you.

Gilbert and George

Yes, it *is* rather a big responsibility
and frankly, not the sort of thing you can trust just
    anybody with,
particularly Hannah Henderson, who can't tie her
    own shoelaces properly
and who once even forgot to invite me
to her birthday party in Year Three.

Ms Forrester said she was looking for somebody
who was not afraid of hard work
because while Gilbert and George are sweethearts,
there's an awful lot to do (apparently) looking after
    gerbils –
even if it is just for the Easter holidays.

You have to clean their cage, give them fresh
    something or other every day,
remember to make sure their door is closed blah blah –
I wasn't really listening, to be honest,
because I was in the middle of the most delicious
    daydream
about having a cuddle with the pair of them.

Anyway, Ms Forrester said she'd pull a name out at
    random
but I suspect she'd rigged it so my name came out –
like I say she couldn't have entrusted Gilbert and
    George to anybody –
so I wasn't surprised to get the job,
although I did scream with excitement for a little while.

And I must say, I have been brilliant at looking after
    them.
I think Gilbert and George are far happier here
at home with me than they are in the classroom.
It's probably to do with not seeing Hannah
    Henderson's stupid face
gurning in at them through the bars every morning.

Imagine Hannah Henderson trying to look after them,
having to remember all the things you have to do,
like making sure you . . . Hang on, that's funny –
Gilbert and George must be playing hide-and-seek
    this morning,
they're usually just there, goofing around

when I bring them their breakfast –

and why is their door open? I'm sure I closed it last
 night.

I *definitely* closed it last night. I might have closed it
 last night.

I did get a little bit distracted by the football, though.

Mum. Mum! Mum! MUM! MUM!!!

CHECK UNDER THE SOFA!

LOOK UNDER THE RUG!

SEARCH THE FIREPLACE!

PEEK IN THAT JUG!

WHAT ABOUT THE PLANT POT?

OR UNDER THAT HAT?

BENEATH THAT BIG CUSHION!

OR THERE, BY THE CAT?

THE CAT, THE CAT, THE CAT!!!!

SHE'S SMACKING HER LIPS!!

SHE'S EATEN GILBERT AND GEORGE!

THAT MUST BE IT!

OH NO! OH NO! OH NO! OH NO!
OH NO! OH NO! OH NO! OH NO!
OH NO! OH NO! OH NO! OH NO!
OH NO! OH NO! OH – sorry, what's that, Mum?

Gilbert and George are in their cage?
Yeah, I knew that. Yeah, of course I did!
It was just a little game I play sometimes called umm…
'The Gerbils Have Escaped'. It's a good game,
it really is. Gilbert and George love it.

By the way, Mum, I was wondering if it would be OK
for Hannah Henderson to come over later?
She could help me play with Gilbert and George.
She might like that. I would too. Or maybe
we could just sit quietly and do a bit of drawing.

Annual Performance Review Meeting with the Family Cat

Good morning! Please do strut inside and take a seat.
No, no, that's fine. You hunker down there.
I didn't really plan on using my arms anyway.

Thanks very much for bothering to come along today.
I do appreciate you must be busy,
what with all the sleeping and everything.

So just to reiterate, the point of this meeting
is to review your performance over the last twelve
    months,
and identify a few goals for next year.

Tell me, what do you enjoy about your current position?
The *sunshine*. I see. Anything else? Feel free to expand.
Oh, you have. Now, don't take this the wrong way,

but I'd like to pick up on a few teensy-weensy areas
for you to work on over the next twelve months.
Firstly, I've received feedback from the rest of the
    family

that you need to be a little bit more of a team player.
Don't get me wrong! It's wonderful to see the initiative
you show in setting your own agenda,

it's just that sometimes you seem more absorbed
in achieving your own personal targets
than anything for the wider team. Which brings me

to the subject of your attitude towards authority.
Now, there's no need to stare at me like that –
that's exactly what I'm talking about.

No, no, no! Of course I have faith in you!
You've made terrific progress this year
and you're a much loved member of the team.

There may have been a few issues when you joined us
but 'Pigeongate' and that incident with next door's
tropical aquarium seem a long time ago now.

Moving on, and thinking ahead to the future,
where do you see yourself in five years' time?
What? You would like to be sitting where I am now?

Oh, hang on, it appears you already are.

Three-Line Poem about the Sounds Coming from Upstairs

You keep loft pigeons?
That explains what the noise is –
Must be a high coo.

You and Your Two-Ton Pet Elephant

The real elephant
in the room,
if you'll beg my pardon,

is why on earth
you don't keep him
in your garden.

Thing of the Past(a)

On the subject of inappropriate pets,
my Auntie Bex had a T-Rex.

His name was Terry (short for Terryannosaurus).
The problem wasn't so much that he terrorized the
    neighbourhood
(although he did – eating six grown-ups and at least
    twelve kids a day,
as well as trampling all over Mrs Tedds' flowerbeds);
it was more that he was such a *dinosaur*.

From TikTok to K-pop, from Pokémon to Xbox –
modern life had passed him by. Terry just couldn't
    get to grips
(in spite of those talons) with FIFA or fidget spinners,
microchips, gastropubs or tanning salons,
and don't get him started on Twenty20 cricket.

He just couldn't stick it. And so, in between rampages,
he would bang on about how things were *so* much
    better in his day
before the mobile phone and body spray,
nasal trimmers and antifreeze. That is, until the day
he discovered . . . mac and cheese.

After that, he was much better.
Sure, he was still partial to the odd neighbour or two
but that was more out of boredom, of having
    something to do.
It somehow made the minutes go faster,
a few hapless appetizers before his cheesy pasta.

My Cat's Previous Eight Lives

In 1969,
as Armstrong and Aldrin packed for the moon and
    headed off on their trip,
my cat had a kip.

In 1851,
when plans for the Great Exhibition were being
    composed,
my cat dozed.

In 1789,
while Louis XVI appraised the mob and realized his
    days were numbered,
my cat slumbered.

In 1533,
after Thomas More refused the Oath and then sadly
    paid the price,
my cat snoozed (and dreamt of mice).

In 1351,
as the Black Death swept,
my cat slept.

In 150,
while Ptolemy did some geometry and got the world
    mapped,
my cat napped.

In 64,
when Rome was burning, Nero fiddling and the
    citizens showed their ire,
my cat curled up by the fire.

In 1323 BC,
after spending the year with both eyes firmly shut,
my cat got buried with King Tut.

Beautiful Plumage

I took her back to the pet shop two weeks later.
'She's not well,' I said, removing the cover from her
    cage.

'How do you know?' asked the pet shop owner.
He looked at me suspiciously from behind his counter.

'She's listless. Just sits there all day, not doing anything.'
'Well, what do you expect?' the pet owner replied.

If truth be told, I did not care much for his manner.
'She's barely said a single word since I got her,' I said.

'That's not unusual,' the pet shop owner said. 'Besides,
what makes you think I can do anything about it?
    I'm not a miracle worker.'

I was finding the man most unhelpful.
'But you sold her to me,' I said. 'She's not well, I'm
    telling you.'

He shrugged. 'Look at her! She's all orange,' I said, shaking the cage at him. 'And crunchy,' I added.

The pet shop man had started to chuckle.
'Why are you laughing?' I said, practically shouting now.

'What's so funny about this?' I repeated.
'I thought you'd said *carrot*,' he said. 'I was sure you said carrot.'

Lab of Love

She's a Labrador in a golden lab coat,
who's conducting lots of tests
to find out ways to make you say
that she's the very best.

She's a Dogtor of Devotedness
with a PhD in love,
peering through her microscope
to see what you're made of.

She's turning up her Bunsen burner
and warming up your heart
then writing down the test results
to plot them in a chart

so that she can find the formula
to know what makes you tick –
what makes you take her to the park
or throw for her a stick

but more than that, she wants to learn
all it is that she can do
to make you happy, to give you joy,
the science behind you.

'Two Dinners' Dennis

is what they call him around here,
because wherever there is food,
'Two Dinners' Dennis will appear.

He has two dinners for breakfast,
two for lunch & two for tea,
sometimes he dines at number nine,
number twelve or thirty-three –

& some days, when he's feeling peckish,
he'll pop into number five
in the hope of some elevenses –
it keeps body & soul alive.

He'll join the barbecue at number two,
or occasionally, on his uppers,
he'll sneak through the door of number twenty-four
& grab a pair of suppers.

Now I'm not saying 'Two Dinners' Dennis
has begun to put on weight
but he can't get through the cat flap
at number twenty-eight

which is a shame because that's where he lives –
he's about the size of a small horse.
I hoist him in, ask if he'd like some food;
he miaows, 'I'm starving – yes, of course.'

Present Company Excepted

Cousin Cora became rather rueful
upon being given a seal
of approval

as her main birthday present.
The seal kept clapping her
wherever she went.

Still, when it came to matters
of the aquatic marine,
it could have been worse.

Her best friend Shareen –
after a mix-up with her parents –
was even more miffed

when she tore open
the wrapping of her birthday gift,
having had her heart set

on a pair of cute tortoises,
only to discover it was a case
of cross porpoises.

Fins aren't what they used to be

Oh, *zut alors*!
It is so unfair,

my poor little fish,
mon petit Pierre

from Normandy, France,
a – *how you say?* – lovely fella,

has gone and damaged
his propeller

and now it seems
he cannot swim.

End of my poem.
La fin of his fin.

The Very Comfy Caterpillow

is furry
and purry,
with three pairs
of legs

& I rest
my head on her
when I go
to bed

Mike

I first met Mike
when he crawled out
from underneath a bunch of bananas
at the supermarket.

I didn't know he was called Mike at the time.
All I knew about him
was that he was big and hairy –
with a big and hairy black body
and eight big and hairy black and orange legs.
Oh, I also knew that he was big.
And rather hairy, too.

He looked like he was lost.
Not lost as if he was used to shopping at the Tesco's
    around the corner
and he'd spent the last ten minutes
trying to locate the deli counter,
but lost as if he'd been teleported to an unfamiliar
    planet,

with different sights and sounds and smells.
I could tell that by the anxious look in his eight eyes.

I thought it for the best
for me to pop him in my pocket
and bring him home with me.
I didn't mention it to Mum.

II

It took Mike a while to settle in.
I suppose that our way of life – school (Monday to
    Friday),
guitar lesson (Saturday morning), *Match of the Day*
    (Sunday morning),
chips (Thursday night tea) etc. –
was very different to the one he was used to.
But as the weeks went by,
he got used to the rhythms of the week,
the geography of my bedroom, the sound of my voice.

And he loved cricket.
I would feed him one, three days a week,
along with the odd mealworm or fly.

We became friends. The best of friends.
We'd chat for hours after lights out,
swapping stories about what we'd been up to that day
(me: French, maths, 40-40-in;
Mike: mainly just sitting still for hours on end),
or we'd talk about our dreams and hopes for the future.

Sometimes, Mike would feel sad
when he thought about home
and how it was too difficult to go back
to where he had come from.

The two of us became inseparable.
I even brought him into school once
and showed him to my friends in the playground at
    lunchtime.
Alice screamed. 'Arrrgh! Tarantula!'
That's rude, I thought. You're a Sagittarius.
None of us are perfect.

I think that was the day before Mum found him.

III

That was fifteen years ago
but I remember it as if it was yesterday:
Mum freaking out; me in tears;
Mike not knowing what was going on.

He'll have to go, Mum said. I couldn't keep him. He
     was dangerous.
He'll kill me, then kill her, and rampage down the
     street.
And living here wasn't good for him, either, she added.
He didn't *belong* here.

But he can't go back, I told Mum after she'd calmed
     down a little.
This is his home now, I said, and as if to prove my point,
Mike crawled slowly up the leg of my jeans and
     settled on my knee,
looking up at Mum
with those eight anxious eyes of his.

We had to make some changes.
There were no more trips to school for Mike.
We went to buy him a proper enclosure,
fitted it out with soil and bark, a big tree branch,
some rocks and a few plants,
and the day Mike moved in,
he began to spin his silk all around his new burrow,
and I swear to you I could make out the words
    'thank you'
among the fine fibres of his web.

Fifteen years. He's still with me now.
He's been with me through school, university
and he's there when I come home from work every
    evening.
We still have those late night chats
once the lights are out
and, sometimes, Mike will think back
to long ago days in a faraway place,
those hazy days before he crawled out to the glare of
    the supermarket lights,
a stranger in a strange land,
and made of it a new life, a new family, a home.

A Spot of Bother

Auntie Nat,
got herself a cat.

Nothing unusual about that,
except this one was huge,
had big sharp teeth,
and was covered in spots.
Lots.

I said to her,
'I don't want to alarm you
but your cat looks rather leopardy –
I think you may be
in jeopardy.'

'Pfff!' Nat said.
'He'll soon change his spots.'
But alas, he did not.

There was a big turn-out
for Auntie Nat's funeral two weeks later,
including all her nephews and nieces.

May she rest in pieces.

The Difference between Cats and Dogs

Dog:

Human lifeform,
You keep me warm
And give me food,
You cater for my every mood.
You give me hugs,
You give me love –
All of this you do for free.
There's nothing you wouldn't do for me,
Whatever the odds.

Therefore, I conclude:
You must be God.

Cat:

Human lifeform,
You keep me warm
And give me food,
You cater for my every mood.
You give me hugs,
You give me love –
All of this you do for free.
There's nothing you wouldn't do for me,
Whatever the odds.

Therefore, I conclude:
I must be God.

For I Will Consider my Chicken, Barbara

For I will consider my chicken, Barbara.

For she is queen of the coop and of regal and stately
stature.

For at the first glimpse of the new day's glory, she
bustles forth about her business.

For first she stretches her legs and wings.

For secondly she enlarges her comb and wattle.

For thirdly she studies her throne in deep
contemplation.

For fourthly she emits a squawk to inform the world
the time has come.

For fifthly she fluffs up and tosses feathers and straw
upon her back.

For sixthly she hunkers down upon her throne and
stills herself.

For seventhly she assumes a look of glassy-eyed
concentration.

For eighthly she raises herself slightly in anticipation
and frowns deeply.

For ninthly she begins her egg song of celebration.

For tenthly she heads off hurriedly in search of food.

For while the corn is plentiful, the day is short and
she is no spring chicken.

For she must peck diligently at the ground and clear
up its scatterings.

For she runs around like a headless chicken, except
for the presence of a head.

For she is hungry and her hunger waits for no one.

For no one gets in the way of Barbara when she is in
this mood.

For she is the answer to the eternal riddle: for second
came the egg, having first come Barbara.

For Barbara must come first always.

For she is of the tribe of tyrannosaurus.

For she possesses a temper to deter the most
fearsome of beasts.

For though she is chicken she fears no fox.

For the fox knows her well and keeps his distance.

For she puffs out her chest and flaps her wings.

For her screech is loud enough to give the dead a
headache.

For her glare could wither a foe from fifty yards.

For, like I say, no one messes with Barbara.

For all that, she is capable of great love and affection.

For every afternoon she runs to greet me off the
school bus.

For though she cannot fly, she is an excellent runner.

For she shakes her tail feathers in happiness when
she sees my feet upon the step.

For she is in need of hugs and to be told that she is
loved.

For she nestles her head into my shoulder.

For she clucks quietly in contentment.

For she tells me stories about how her day and
listens attentively, in turn, to mine.

For we are blessed to have each other.

For she is first in my pecking order and I am first in
hers.

For she is funny and feisty and loyal and loving.

For she is Barbara.

Cats and Dogs: Peace Treaty

1. This treaty recognizes the independence of cats. This includes their right to self-determination, self-government, and doing pretty much whatever they want, wherever they want to do it, at any time they would like.

2. In return, cats have agreed to let sleeping dogs lie.

3. All weapons must be surrendered. Cats have until 12 o'clock tonight to retract their claws, while the baring of fangs is now outlawed: any dogs in breach of this will be at risk of surrendering their status as a very good boy or a very good girl.

4. Both cats and dogs are to respect the borders and boundaries laid out by The Domicile Commission. All captured territory, including the comfy armchair in the sitting room and the piece of carpet in front of the fire, shall be restored to its original status and its neutrality guaranteed.

5. Any possessions captured by either side must be returned to their original owners. This may include (but not be limited to): chewsticks, catnip, a selection of bones, two packets of tuna-flavoured Dreamies, an assortment of balls and sticks, three dog leads, an old brown slipper, a dead mouse that was under the sofa that morning, one scratching post, and a squeaky toy commonly known as Gerald the Elephant.

6. In the event of further disagreements or disputes, all matters should be brought for consideration and adjudication by Mr Hoppy McHopperton, current chair-rabbit of the United Pets League.

7. The terms of this treaty will come into effect from midnight tonight and be forgotten approximately two hours later.

The Dog Year Myth

'One human year does not equal seven dog years.
No one knows where the dog years myth came from,
but experts agree that it's simply not true.'
   The Smithsonian Magazine

Nice try, scientists.
But do not dare to take away
my dog years.

And while we're at it,
you can leave alone my cat years,
my rabbit years,
my goldfish years, too.

There's some new maths in town –
one dog year (or cat year, rabbit year etc.)
is equal to
one human year of happiness.

It's a pet theory of mine;
good luck in trying to disprove that.

Index of First Lines

Out now!

50 Ways
to Score
a Goal
and other
football poems
Brian
Bilston

Football Is ...

Football is ...
Football is a wiggle of the hips
Football is a whistle to the lips
Football is late-night fish and chips
Football is

Football is an unwritten poem
Football is trousers in need of sewing
Football is days off when it's snowing
Football is

Football is a scrambled goal line clearance
Football is a school bell disappearance
Football is a blind adherence
Football is

Football is a language that's universal
Football is a perfect centre circle
Football's the real thing not a rehearsal
Football is

Football is a door without need of a key
Football is one thing for you, another for me
Football is whatever you want it to be
Football is ...

Fifty Ways to Score a Goal

tap in, toe poke, thunderbolt,
backheel, nutmeg, stinger,
glancing header, mis-hit cross,
rebound, blaster, zinger

goalkeeping blunder, penalty,
curler, sidefoot, prod,
scissors, volley (full and half)
scorcher, Hand of God

rocket, drill, fire, lash it in,
bundle, drive, stab, chip,
screamer, belter, slam, caress,
bum, shin, chin, knee, hip

diving header, outrageous lob,
deflection, quick free-kick,
finesse, stroke, steer, walk it in,
dink, punt, slot and flick